W9-BUA-467

Hotel Deep

KURT CYRUS

Hotel Deep

LIGHT VERSE FROM DARK WATER

HARCOURT, INC.
Orlando Austin New York San Diego Toronto London
Printed in Singapore

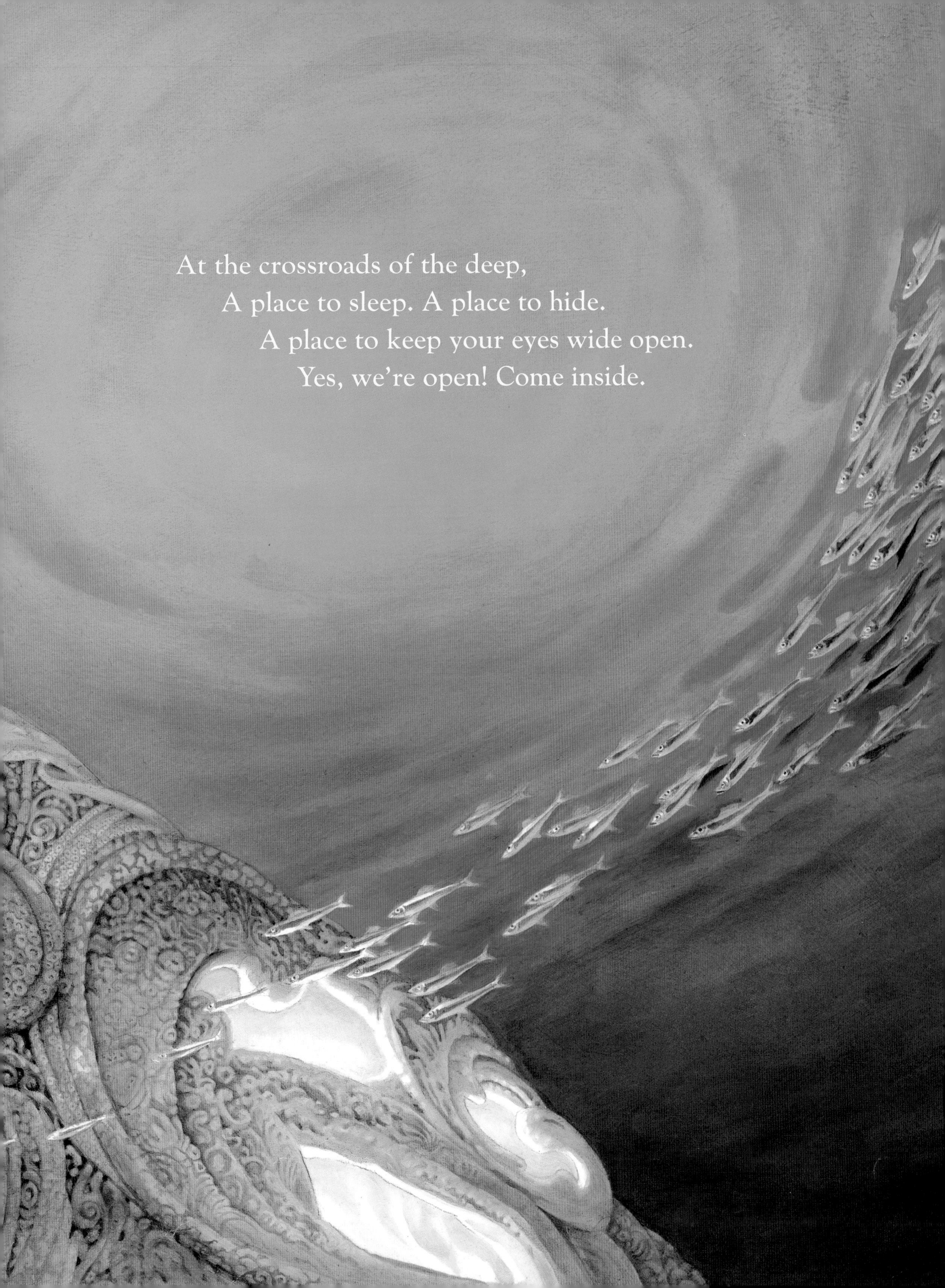

At the crossroads of the deep,
A place to sleep. A place to hide.
A place to keep your eyes wide open.
Yes, we're open! Come inside.

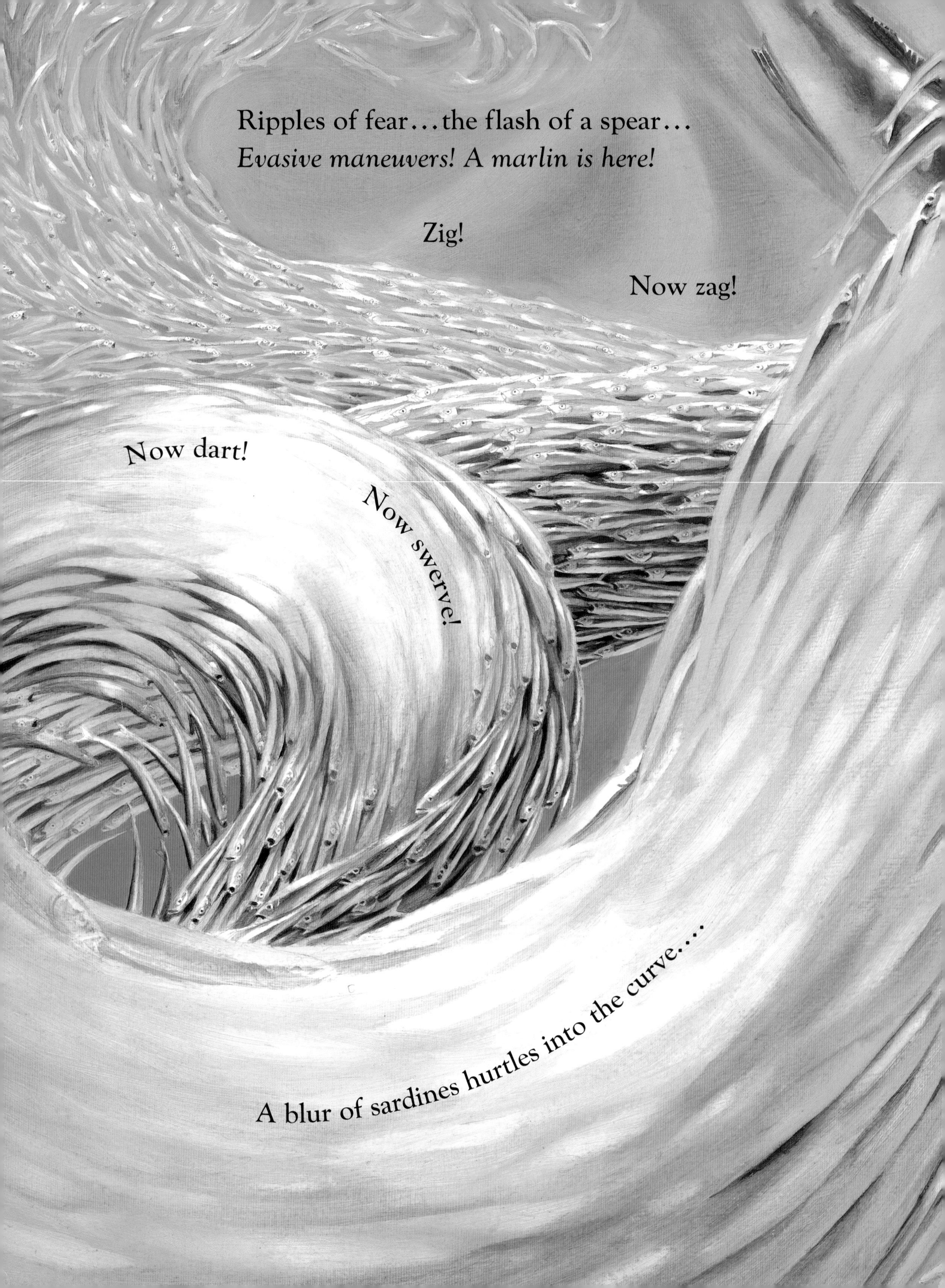

Ripples of fear... the flash of a spear...
Evasive maneuvers! A marlin is here!

Zig!

Now zag!

Now dart!

Now swerve!

A blur of sardines hurtles into the curve....

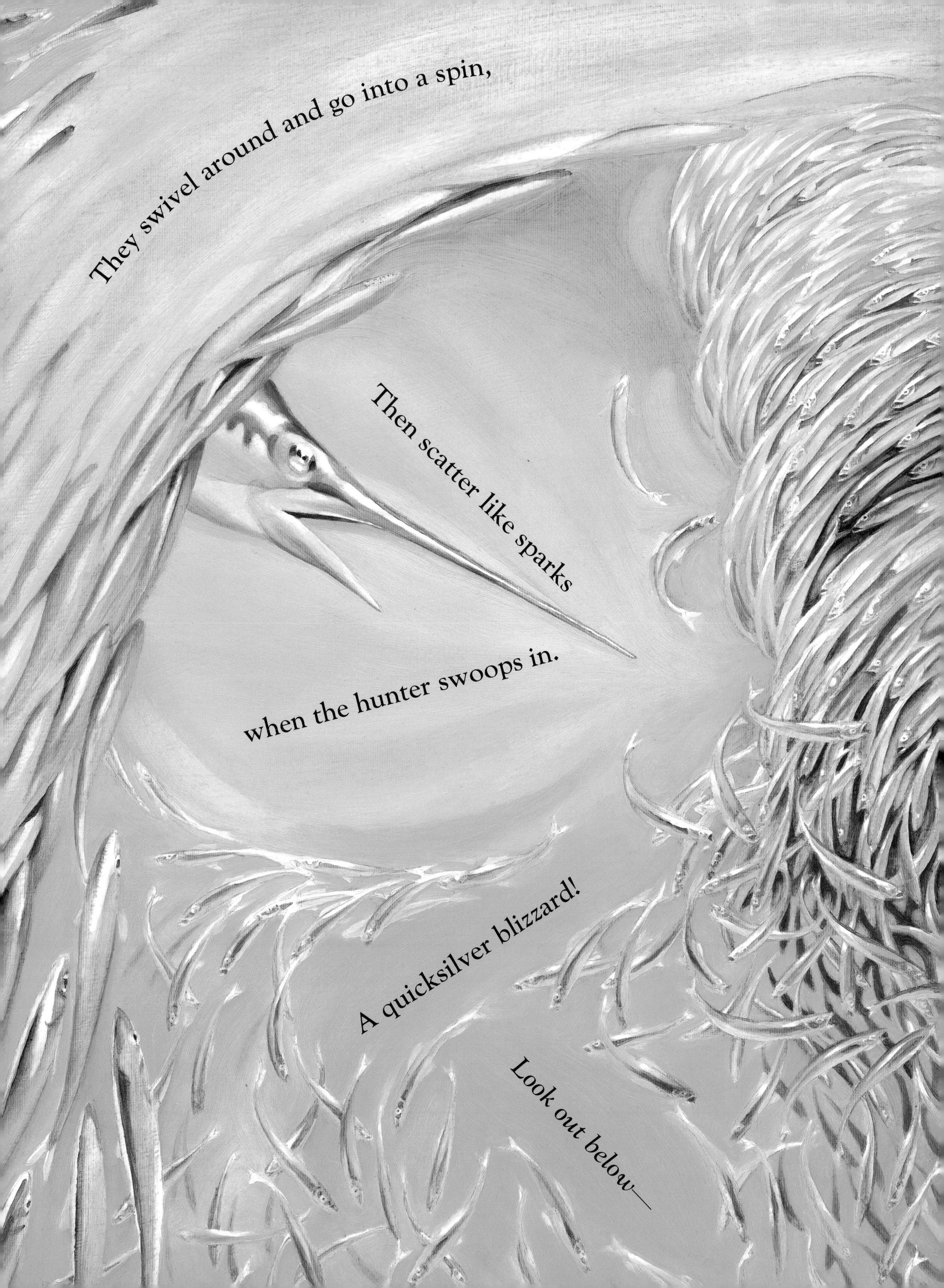

They swivel around and go into a spin,
Then scatter like sparks
when the hunter swoops in.
A quicksilver blizzard!
Look out below—

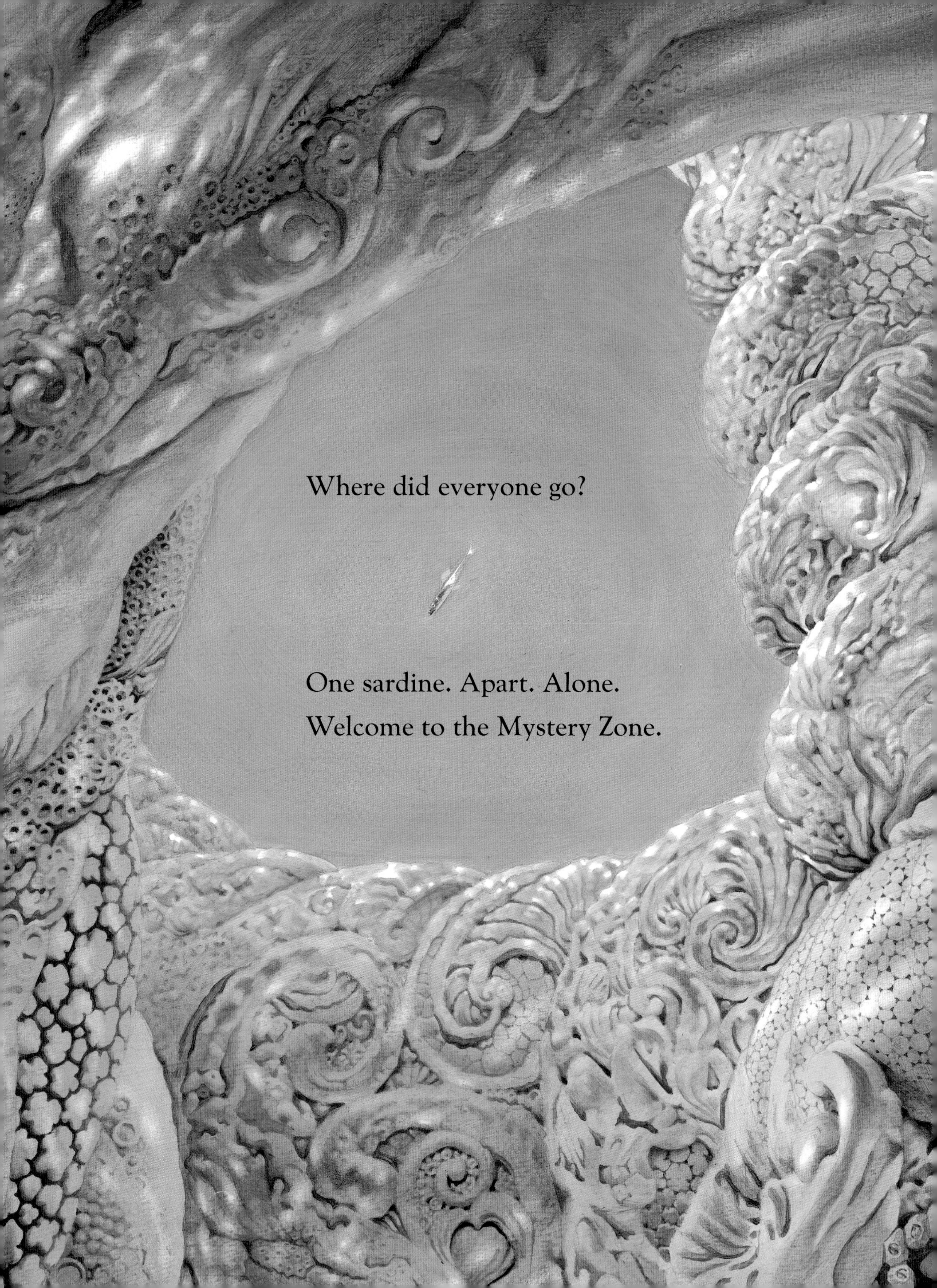
Where did everyone go?
One sardine. Apart. Alone.
Welcome to the Mystery Zone.

How do you do?
Who do you eat?
Have you been chased?
Glad we could meet.
How do you taste?
How do you do?
Won't it be wonderful,
swallowing you?

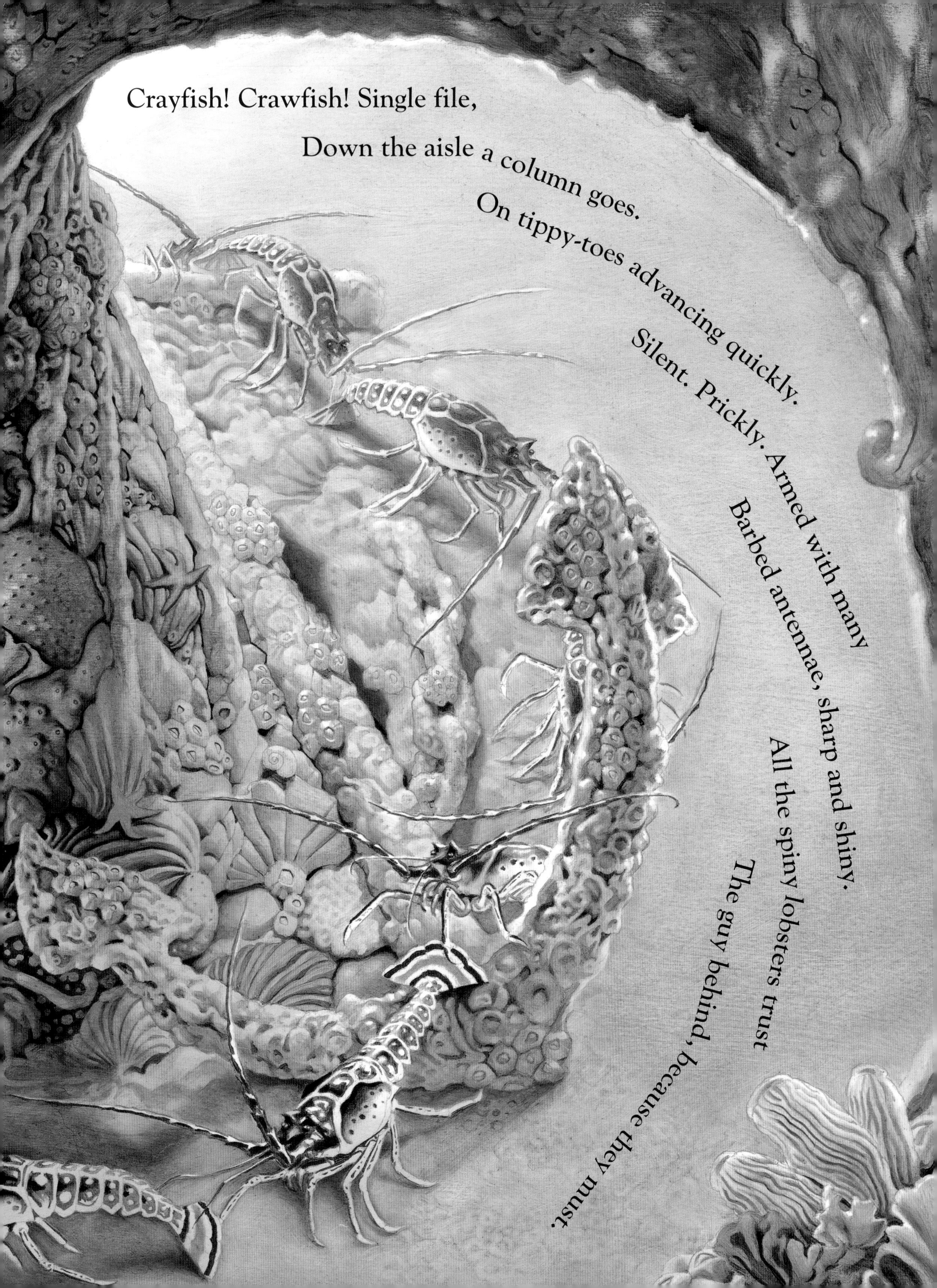

Crayfish! Crawfish! Single file,
Down the aisle a column goes.
On tippy-toes advancing quickly.
Silent. Prickly. Armed with many
Barbed antennae, sharp and shiny.
All the spiny lobsters trust
The guy behind, because they must.

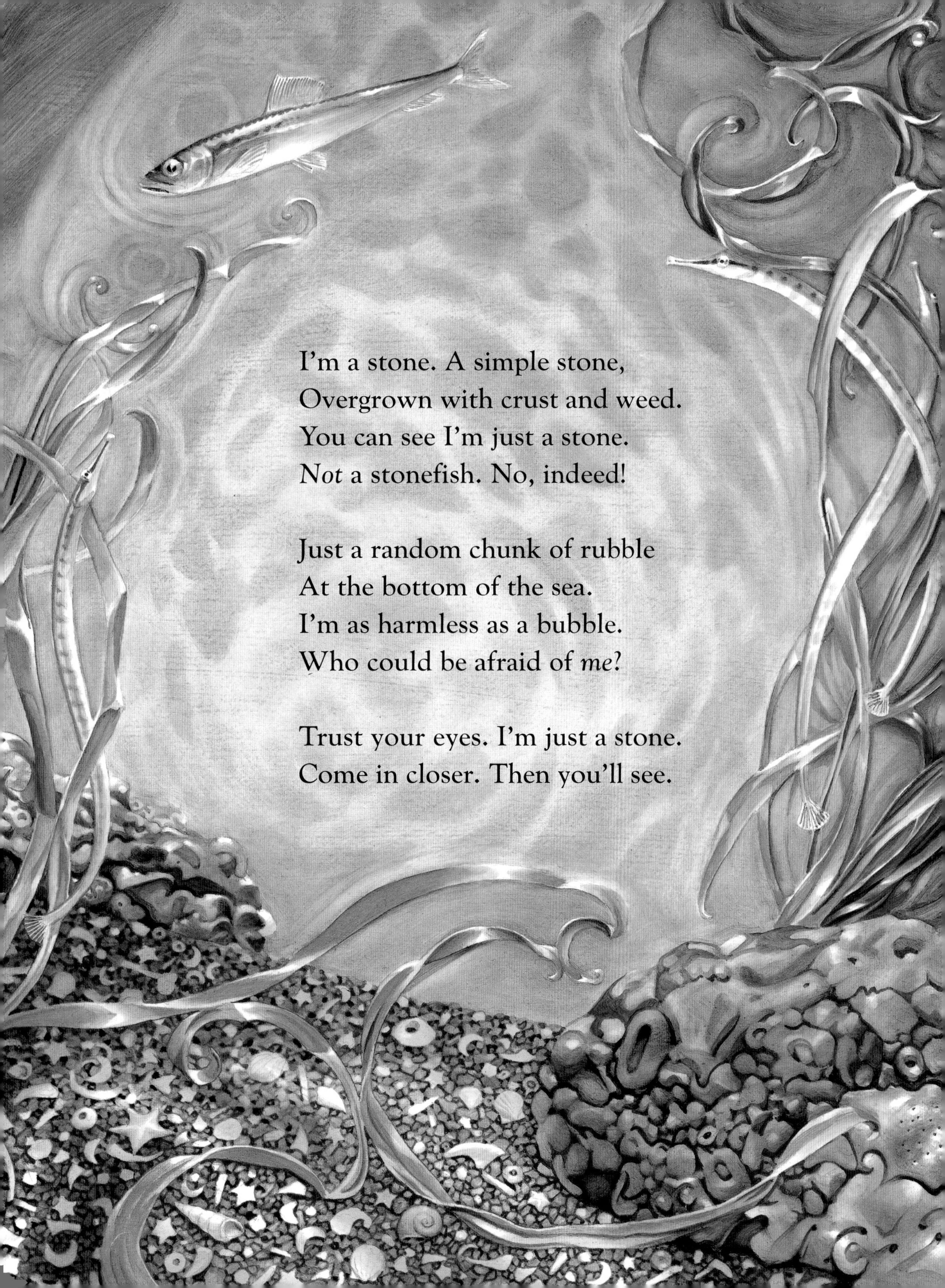

I'm a stone. A simple stone,
Overgrown with crust and weed.
You can see I'm just a stone.
Not a stonefish. No, indeed!

Just a random chunk of rubble
At the bottom of the sea.
I'm as harmless as a bubble.
Who could be afraid of *me*?

Trust your eyes. I'm just a stone.
Come in closer. Then you'll see.

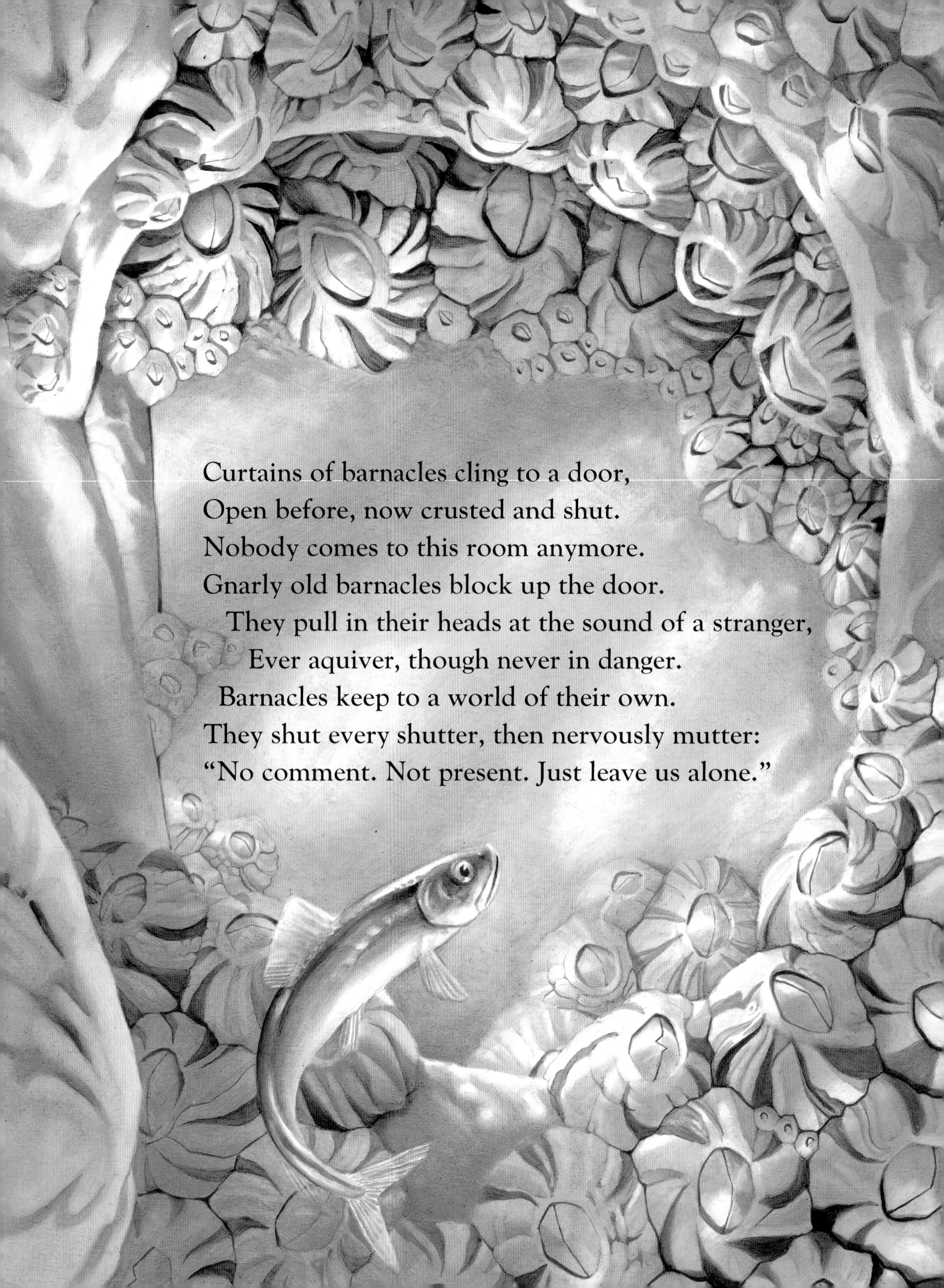

Curtains of barnacles cling to a door,
Open before, now crusted and shut.
Nobody comes to this room anymore.
Gnarly old barnacles block up the door.
They pull in their heads at the sound of a stranger,
Ever aquiver, though never in danger.
Barnacles keep to a world of their own.
They shut every shutter, then nervously mutter:
"No comment. Not present. Just leave us alone."

The angulated wentletrap, in alabaster white,
Is one of many enemies to any sea anemone.
If it sees anemones, it always takes a bite.
(Anemones regenerate, so everything's all right.)

At a glance, a calico scallop
Looks to lack a thing or two:
No fins to swim, no legs to gallop.
If you scare a calico scallop,
What does the scallop do?

Well…

…it startles! It snaps!
It claps, and it claps, and goes
swooooooping around
and then loooooooooping
the loop, as it
pumping and pitching and

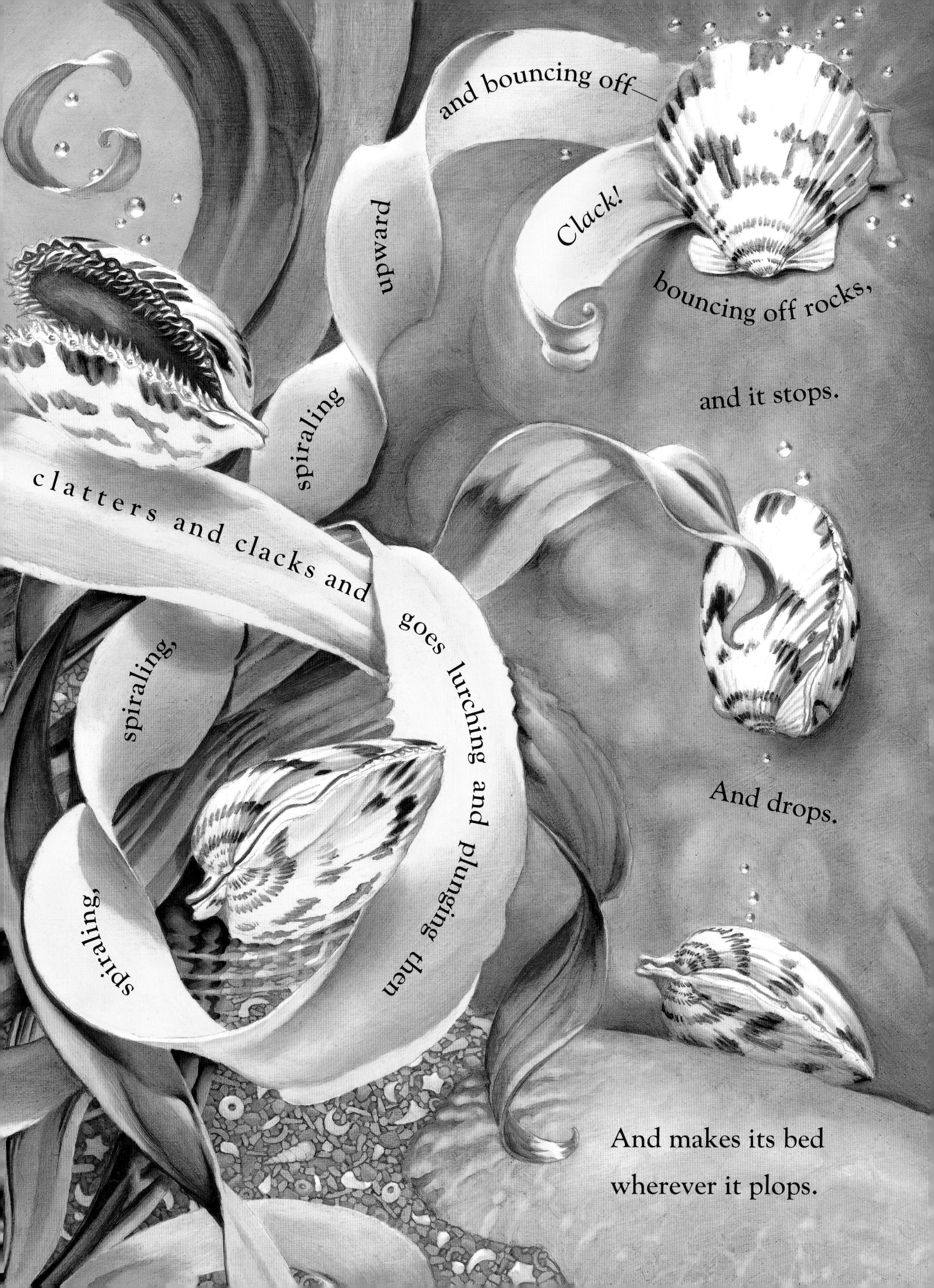
clatters and clacks and
goes lurching and plunging then
spiraling,
spiraling,
spiraling
upward
and bouncing off—
Clack!
bouncing off rocks,
and it stops.
And drops.
And makes its bed
wherever it plops.

In a small, secluded den,
An octopus's eggs are hung.
She gently strokes them now and then.
The mother never leaves her young.

She never eats. She doesn't stray.
She watches with unblinking eyes.
And when they've hatched and swum away,
Among the scuttled eggs she dies.

The angler flaps her fleshy flap.
A shrimp comes in. The jaws go *snap*!
The angler doesn't have a clue
Why shrimp come in. They simply do.
And so she eats them. Wouldn't you?

The belch of a blowfish. The bark of a seal.
The murmuring turn of the tide.
The walloping, wallowing yawn of an eel.
The silence of ships that have died.
Ripples come racing on crystal-blue rollers
With tidings from far and wide.

When waves of fear roll up my back,

I gulp and gulp. My body fills.

I swell into a prickly sack,

Bulging out at the gills.

A billowing bladder of water, that's me. I do what I wish, and I dish it out double!

Look out! I can whip any fish in the sea!

Not that I'm looking for trouble…

It's the fate of every flounder.
First of all, she'll travel…

Then her face will twist around her…

Till she lies, a twenty-pounder,
Sideways in the gravel.

It isn't a dance. It isn't romance.
They're clenched in a grip-lock grab,
With never a chance to retreat *or* advance.
There's no letting go of a crab.

Slow-moving paddleboats rowing away.
Turtles away! So long.
So long is the journey you're starting today—
It's time you were going. We wish you could stay.
The ends of the ocean lie far, far away.
So, turtles away! So long.

Lost and lean, a lone sardine
Haunts the doorways of the sea.
"Please, has anybody seen
A million other fish like me?"

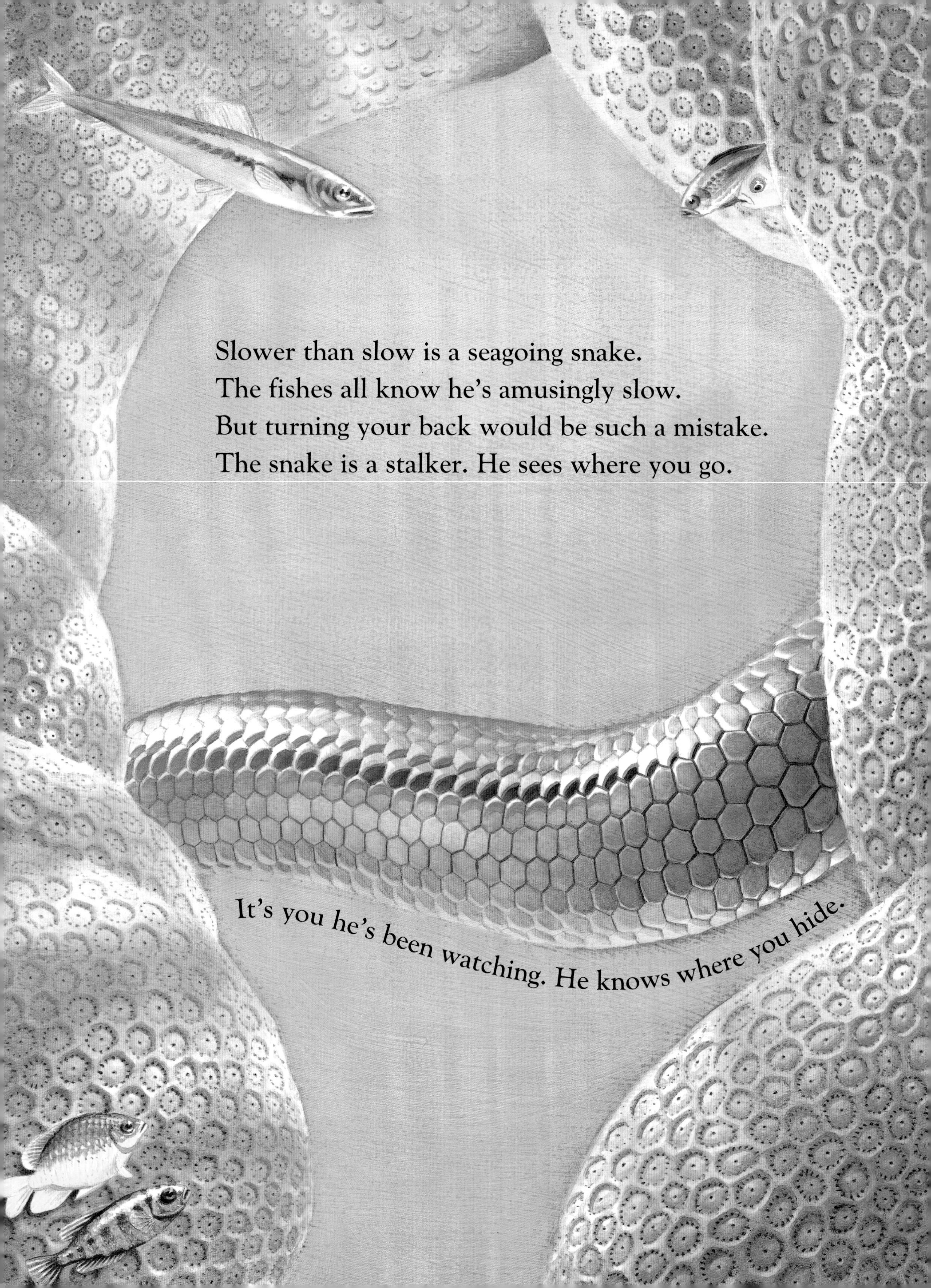

Slower than slow is a seagoing snake.
The fishes all know he's amusingly slow.
But turning your back would be such a mistake.
The snake is a stalker. He sees where you go.

It's you he's been watching. He knows where you hide.

He saw you come in….

He may be inside….

Around any corner…

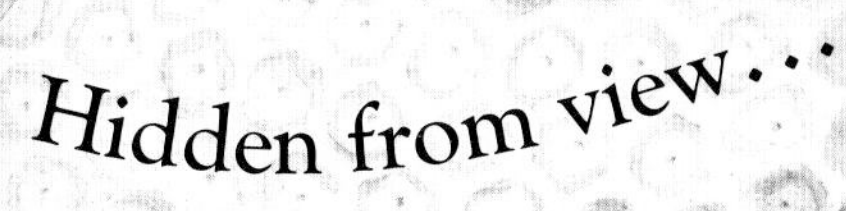

Hidden from view…

He's somewhere….

He's nowhere….

He's here.

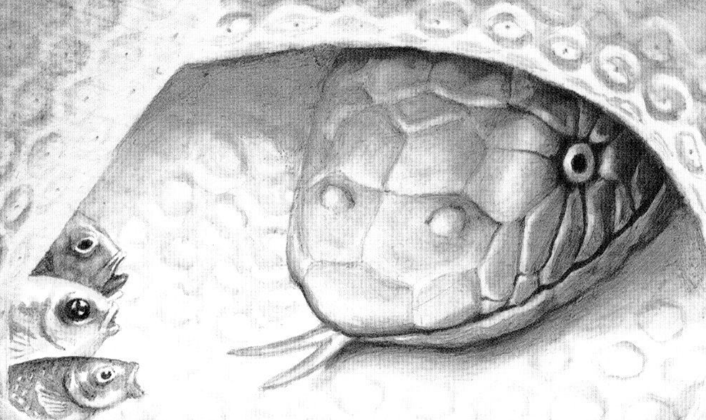

Peekaboo!

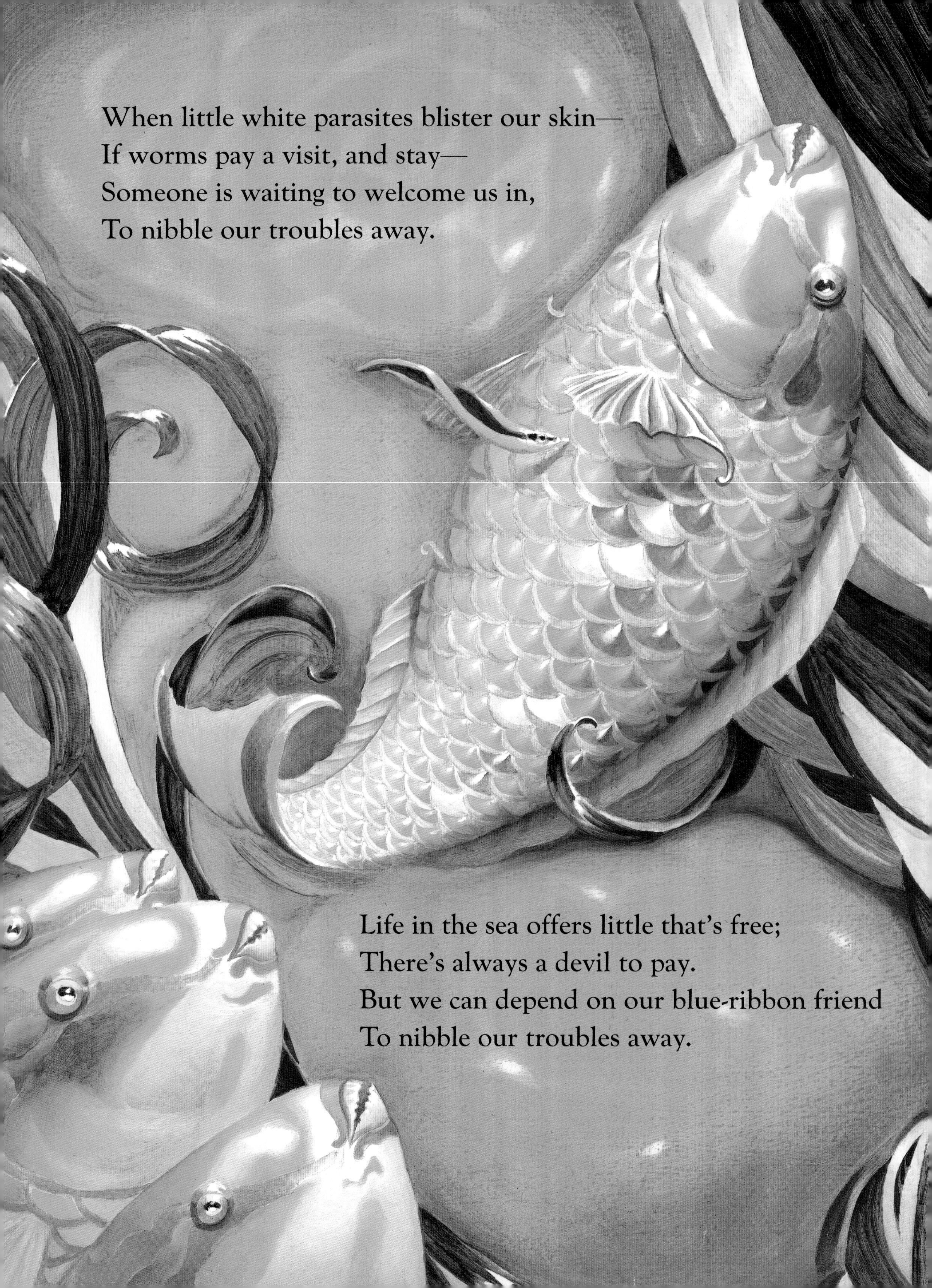

When little white parasites blister our skin—
If worms pay a visit, and stay—
Someone is waiting to welcome us in,
To nibble our troubles away.

Life in the sea offers little that's free;
There's always a devil to pay.
But we can depend on our blue-ribbon friend
To nibble our troubles away.

Crayfish! Crawfish! Never slowing.
Must be going. Must be gone.
Marching on, antennae twirling.
Through a swirling seaweed curtain.
Never certain what will follow.
All are swallowed by the sea,
Swallowed up in mystery.

Silent night. Deepest night.
Tiny lights, like stars in motion,
Twinkle in and out of sight.
Has the sky become the ocean?

Stars that gobble. Stars that bite.
Twinkle, twinkle, little nipper.
Watch those ripples. Douse that light.
Here comes deep-sea Jack the Ripper.

When you wish upon a star,
Wish it won't know where you are.

Around and around in a flash and a swish—
A fish is a rock is a plant is a fish.
Mackerel, manatee, halibut, hake,
Oh, what a crazy mosaic we make!
A puzzle, a dazzle of dizzy surprises,
A jumbled-up tangle of colors and sizes.
Throw them together and give them a shake—
Mackerel, manatee, halibut...

...sardines?

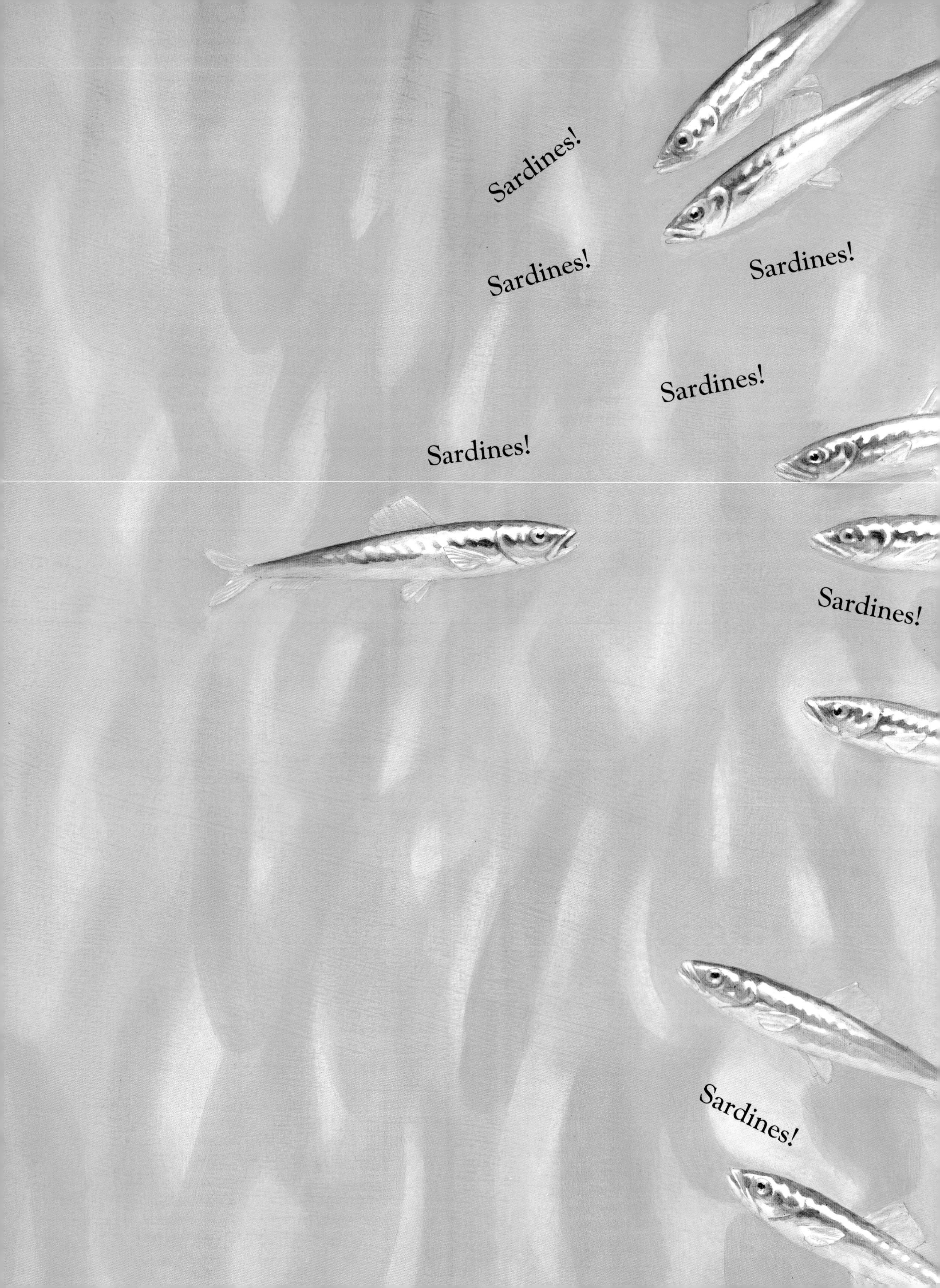
Sardines!
Sardines!
Sardines!
Sardines!
Sardines!
Sardines!
Sardines!

Sardines!

Sardines!

Sardines!

Sardines!

Sardines!

Sardines!

Sardines!

Sardines!

Sardines!

Sardines!

Sardines!

Sardines!

Sardines!

Sardines!

Sardines!

Sardines!

Sardines!

Sardines!

Sardines!

Sardines!

Sardines!

Sardines!

Sardines!

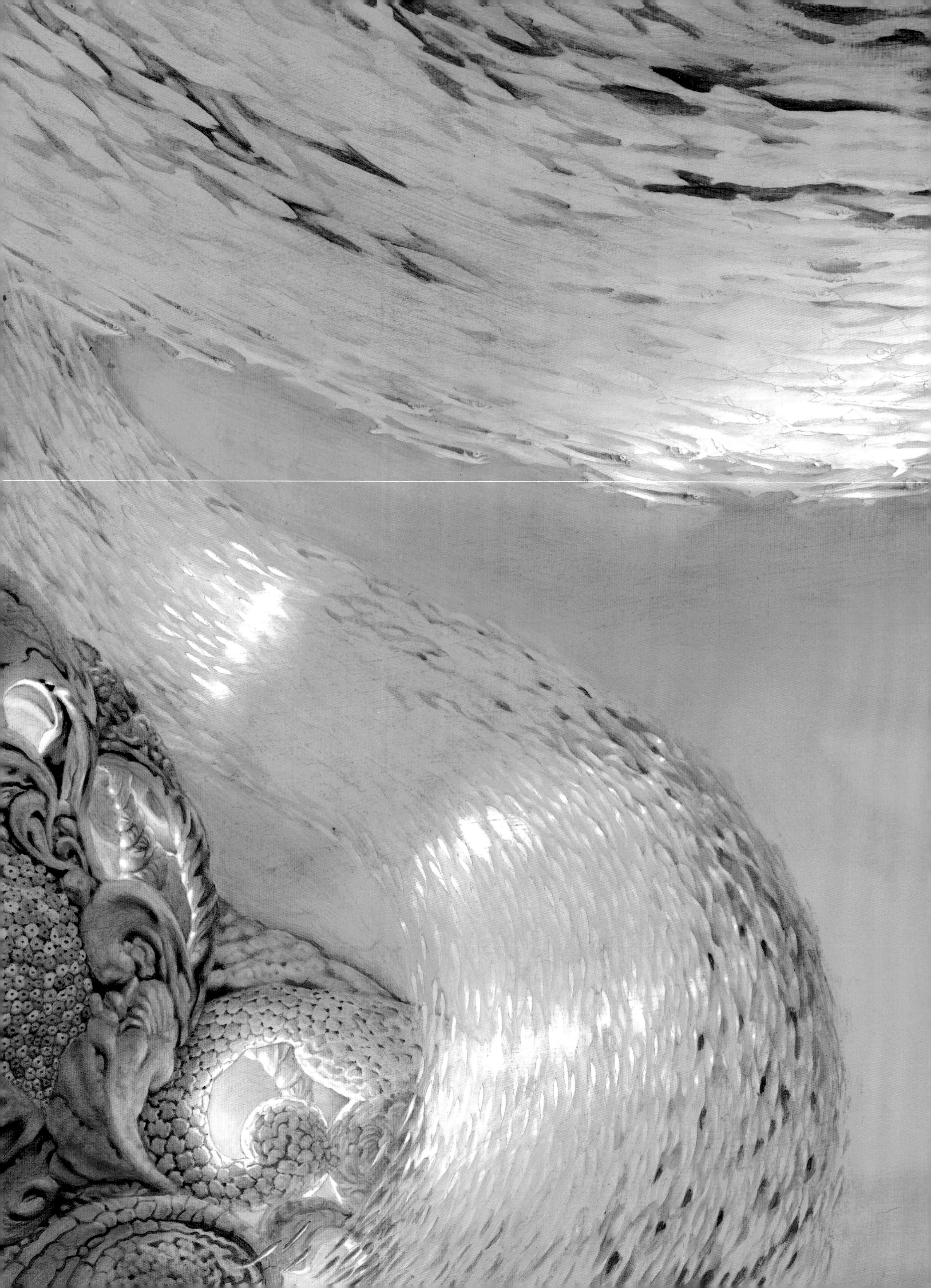

Up we go. Away we glide.
Around the world we sweep!
Swirling currents, rising tide;
Cheek to cheek again, we'll ride
The crossroads of the deep.

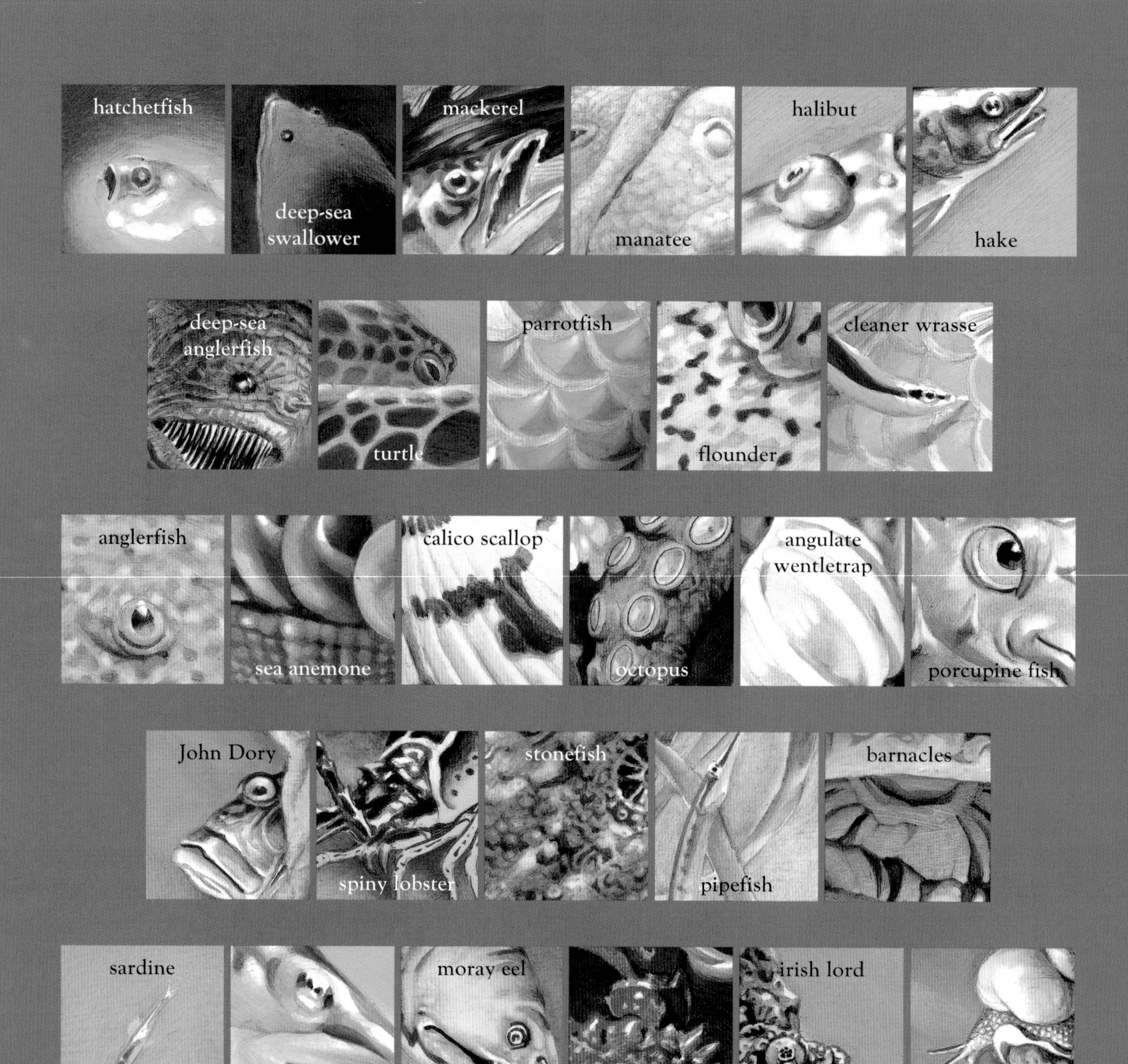

www.HarcourtBooks.com
Library of Congress Cataloging-in-Publication Data
Cyrus, Kurt.
Hotel deep: light verse from dark water / Kurt Cyrus. p. cm.
1. Marine animals—Juvenile poetry. 2. Children's poetry, American. 3. Ocean—Juvenile poetry.
[1. American poetry. 2. Marine animals—Poetry. 3. Ocean—Poetry.] I. Title.
PS3553.Y49H68 2005 811'.6—dc22 2003025999 ISBN 0-15-216771-4

First edition
A C E G H F D B

Color separations by Bright Arts Ltd., Hong Kong Printed and bound by Tien Wah Press, Singapore
This book was printed on totally chlorine-free Stora Enso Matte paper. The display lettering was created by John Stevens.
Production supervision by Ginger Boyer Designed by Kurt Cyrus and Judythe Sieck